"This is a book to be sipped and savore[d]. With an economy of words, Rachel cut[s] straight to the deep—to the reassurances and revelations that release inner pressure valves, giving you room to breathe, to smile, to let yourself gloriously be."

Jen Lee, filmmaker and co-author of *The 10 Letters Project*

The Great Green Okayness is bursting with light and goodness. Rachel is the best listener we have ever met in our lives. In her presence, you feel really seen and heard. This feeling is the heart of her book. Reading it brings you back home to your glorious magnificence! We love it so much!"

Lori Portka and Liv Lane, co-authors of *Infinite Purpose*

"We are constantly bombarded with messages, good and bad, about who we are and our place in world. Rachel Awes teaches us how to take contro[l] those messages by being kind to ourselves. *The G[reat] Green Okayness* is a delightfully illustrated guide to se[e] acceptance and finding joy. I LOVE this book!"

Elizabeth Ries, Twin Cities television and radio personalit[y]

"*The Great Green Okayness* is inspiringly beautiful and provocative. Rachel's stories, along with her magical drawings, promote self-reflection that lingers long after one has finished reading its pages. An important book with an infinitely important message: You are not a work in progress. You are a beautiful you."

Colleen Baldrica, author of *Tree Spirited Woman*

"*The Great Green Okayness* is an uncommon book. Reading it is a revelation, an opening to the goodness within that we may scarcely dare to believe in. Rachel Awes sees our innocence, believes in our innate goodness, and guides the reader, like a master poet, to embrace life's great work: the embodiment of love."

Henry Emmons, MD, author of *The Chemistry of Joy*, *The Chemistry of Calm*, and *Staying Sharp*

THE
GREAT GREEN
Okayness

Rachel Awes

THE
GREAT GREEN
Okayness

A field guide to seeing your uncommon magnificence

Rachel Awes, M.A., L.P.

WISE Ink
CREATIVE ★ PUBLISHING

ISBN 13: 978-1-63489-021-2

Library of Congress Catalog Number: 2015959144

Printed in the United States of America
First Printing: 2016

20   19   18   17   16   5   4   3   2   1

Cover and interior design by James Monroe Design LLC.

Wise Ink, Inc.
837 Glenwood Avenue
Minneapolis, MN 55405

www.wiseinkpub.com

To order, please visit rachelawes.com.
Reseller discounts available.

This land was made for you and me.

—Woody Guthrie,
American folk singer and songwriter

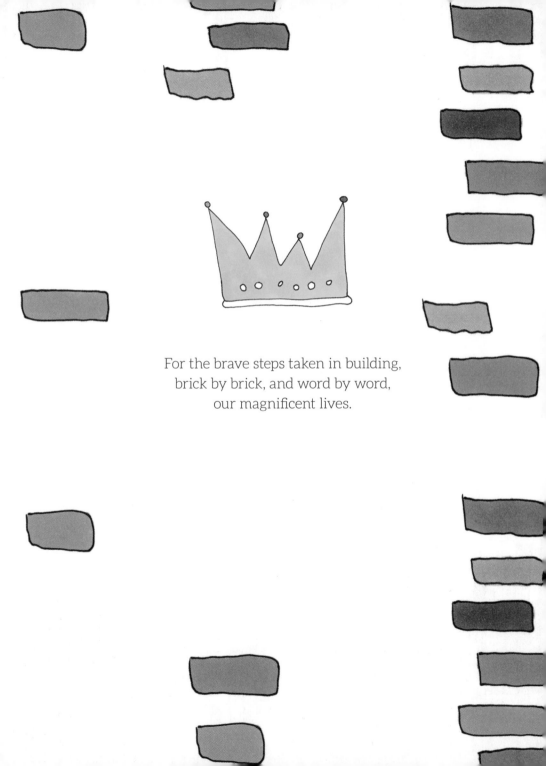

For the brave steps taken in building,
brick by brick, and word by word,
our magnificent lives.

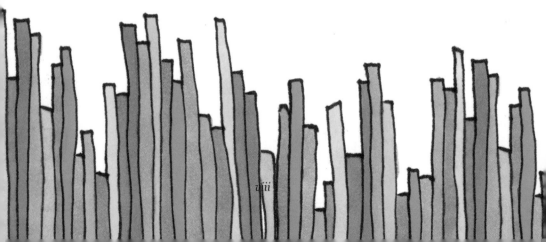

Introduction

I have become an uncommon physician of the heart, in that the therapy room has become my most comfortable room. We get to the real stuff here—and what's real turns out to hold the deepest ease, and furthermore allows people to crack open with beauty right before me. I see them. And I see you. And this realization has changed everything.

One of these beautiful clients, told me about a place she envisioned called The Great Green Okayness. She described it as a great field, ultimately within ourselves, where we are unconditionally accepted. In such a place, we can peaceably see our whole lives without judgment. All our anger and all our joy exist here. While this book is filled with many stories, it seemed most fitting to lift this one into the title. Seeing your whole life as beautiful is this book's overarching invitation. The Great Green Okayness emerged as the expanse to hold all these stories—and to hold all of you. Its story is placed into the middle of the book, like a heart. The place we beat and belong.

In these pages, you will find sixty-three stories, encouraging sight of your boundless worth, substance, and glory. A traditional illustrated field guide serves to identify the wildlife around you, and this one is designed to identify the wildlife **within** you. Through storytelling, my intent is to show YOU to you—the great landscape of yourself. Concrete guidance is also woven throughout select passages. Personal reflection and book club questions can be found in the back to help implement the inspiration into your life. Each page is designed to be an elephantine message of your uncommon magnificence. A homecoming. A cumulative avalanche of love for you.

I am so glad you are here. Your glory bedazzles.

With great love and welcome,

Rachel

psychologist, author, speaker, and art playgroundist

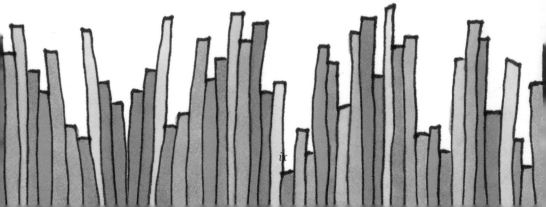

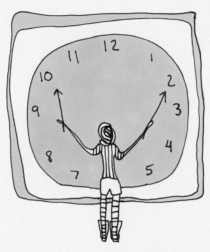

Bright Yellow

"I don't want to take up an hour that someone else may need more than I do" is a message I hear more times than I can count. Here is the thing, tender hearts. No one needs to qualify for healing, transformation, care, and love. Applications are not being taken. You are already accepted and always have been. When did you begin questioning it? Age seven, nine, twelve? That whatever-age-old you were needs all your love. For the record, you have a place in my room, on my block, and in this world. Take up the hour. Breathe into the room. Fill this space with your full breath. Become the bright yellow lion of yourself. Stand your ground. Roar.

1

I See Your Light

A word breaks. Tears run. Eyes dart away. Arms cross. Your coat is still on. What are in all those pockets? What is still zippered in? I don't have any idea what it is like to be in there. I don't really know a thing, except for **the blazing light that is touching my eye.** It's streaming through all of your cracks and filling the entire room.

Your Beauty Stuns Me

One of my clients said that red and purple are her favorite colors. I was struck by how those colors compose the outer edges of a rainbow. And then my mind became transfixed. It was difficult to hear anything else. I was a deer in the headlights. Time stopped. The thing is, I **want** to cooperate with the colors. I **wish** to be stunned by the beauty you speak of and absorb it all for a while. Might you also consider such a place to dwell? **It's not so bad to be stuck in a rainbow.**

You Are More

You are the swift cheetah, the strong lion, the intuitive giraffe, and the dressed-up zebra. You are all of Africa. This whole wide world. You are entirely, all of you. A client told me she was a bear. **We are all more than what we appear.**

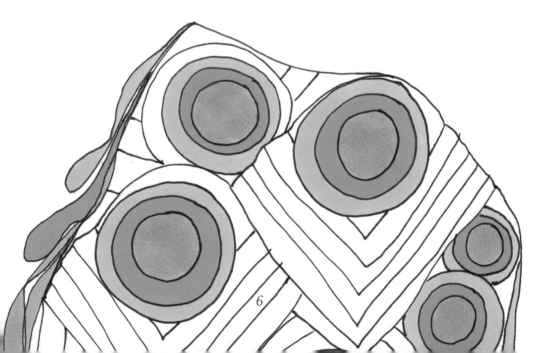

We are all more than what we appear.

What if you thought about yourself as you think of the great redwood forest?

Leap and Believe It

We often imagine our progression in steps. We think that in order to get someplace, we need a lengthy itinerary, a poster size connect-the-dots diagram, and a doctorate degree's amount of instruction. While sometimes this way of thinking is useful, because it really does help us to drive from one place to another, it can also hinder. Take the goal of achieving your fabulousness, for example. **What if you thought about yourself as you think of the great redwood forest?** What if you didn't dissect every little thing and just knew yourself to be fabulous? What if, like faith, there were no more steps but to believe?

Seeing Will Not Hurt You

Our greatest teacher can come in the very thought that scares us the most. We can gain wisdom from our deepest psyche. Such a place will not bring harm. **Are you willing to take another look? To pick up your magic machete and clear the overgrown path? If so, your deep-jungle truth will be given with love.** A client told me that her body was held tightly for years. When she thought of her life, it felt like there was a tiger in her boat, and she needed to be vigilant. The turning point came when she became curious if there was something missing in her vision. It helped her to relax her body and lie down, as she peered back into her life. We sat together in silence for a time, and then her tears streamed. She had been mistaken. It was a lion. And furthermore, if there had been danger, it would have happened by now. The animal had been there to protect her all along.

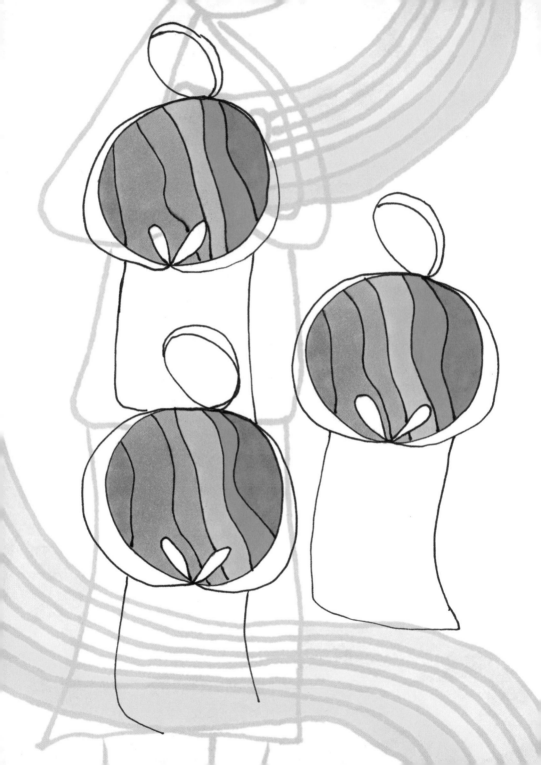

Your Worth Is Unlimited

I find myself having this conversation repeatedly: we all desire to be loved fully, yet sometimes that love comes from key people in our lives in a more limited capacity. We then jump to the conclusion that our worth is limited. Here is the thing. **Our worth does not exist in equal proportion to other people's ability to let us know they love us. Our worth is unlimited.**

Your Heart Is Golden

We are social creatures and fancy feeling treasured. We want evidence of our worth and crave validation. To consider the alternative is crushing. To conceive rejection, ruinous. We can all take heart, however, because **science reveals rich news.** Our bodies house gold. It is most concentrated around the edges of the human heart. Your gold wants to be known and to bring attention to your heart. Gold furthermore frames it, confirming your value.

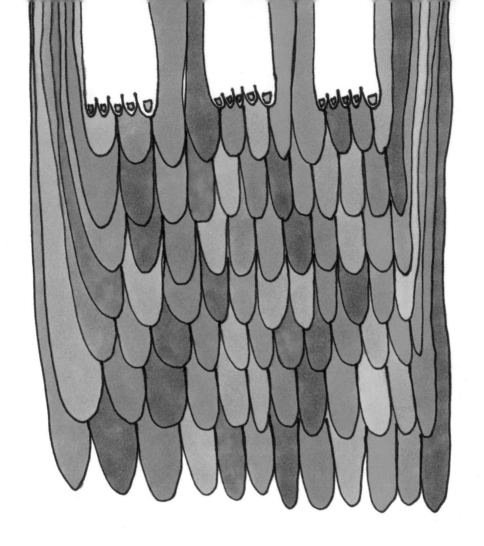

With all her
readiness and order

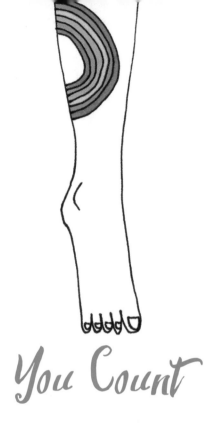

You Count

A new client walked in, and I loved her instantly. Maybe it was the way she kept apologizing or the way she was ready with her insurance information and her organized story to report. Or maybe it was because of how heartbreakingly tender her heart was. Deeper into the hour, she confessed to not being at the point in her life where she wants to be. Of course, this must be what brought her here. **With all her readiness and order, she had missed an important figure. Herself.** She counts. We all do. The hairs on our head. Our fingers and our toes. Our heartbeats. This is where we relax into freedom and how our words change from not being where we want to be, to being exactly where we want.

Your Real Self Is Awesome

You, who grew up with an alcoholic dad, a mom who didn't protect you, a brother who said mean things, a sister who died, friends who rejected you, a girlfriend who broke your heart, and a house that burned down. You, who didn't feel smart in school, weren't chosen in gym class, and weren't asked out to prom. You, who need to feel a sense of purpose, want love badly, and know you are worth something. Be assured, you are not alone. **Some version of these stories course through all our veins.** They don't make you less than—they make you real. Let's sit together in the middle of all your tales because I have something to tell you. Here it is, my real friend: you are a pile of awesome. Your unmet thirst and vulnerability mean that you want love and don't want to be hurt. They mean nothing more than that. Your deep beauty is a fully different matter.

19

enough of the delicate flower bullshit.

Evidence Exists of Your Strength

We can't be strong one moment and then claim we are not that same person in the next. A client taught me this. She is a teacher and told her student who was fretting about something **"enough of the delicate flower bullshit."** She said this because the student had previously shared stories of being remarkably brave. This same confrontation became relevant in my hour with this client, and I told her, "enough of the delicate flower bullshit." Of course, this same confrontation is relevant for us all. I have seen your strength, and there is no going back.

Keep Dressing Up for the Fire

What does it take to get to the other side of something? To get to the finish line of quilt making, child-raising, book writing, field plowing, wedding planning, a full day? It can feel impossible to get through and face all that rises up in us: resistance, fear, discouragement, doubt, and so on. We can be fooled into thinking the goal isn't worth it. It can be easy to forget what is required of us. One client was grappling with this very thing. His freedom came in the form of a memory of his grandpa who used to speak of how making something works. **Creation involves unraveling, swearing, and then, and only then, a move into something new.** It is not all daisies, sweet friends. As you set out to conquer your destiny, you must first anticipate the fire, dress appropriately, and then, and only then, walk on through.

Equip Yourself with Language that Holds You

As our session was coming to a close, a client told me he fluctuates from thinking of himself as a genius in one moment to an idiot in another. I proposed he consider a third option: use a word to hold all his vulnerability and all his brightness. I suggested the alternative of **precious**. It is imperative work to find language that accurately holds our being. **Climb out of ABCs that confine and find words that are big enough.** Your precious heart is waiting.

Intertwine Encouragement into Your Daily Rituals

A client chose "I matter" as her work computer's password to remind her daily of her worth. (Her password is actually slightly different from this, but I didn't want to bust her code). **So much is possible in our daily rituals, and we can maximize them for our greatest good.** We can put reminders on our phone that we are good enough. Write "well done" on our tube of toothpaste. Include a note in our children's lunch bag about how wonderful they are. The possibilities are endless. My heart might burst just thinking of it.

So much is possible in our daily rituals, and we can maximize them for our greatest good.

this is it

Be grateful for What Already Is

With each step as she ran, she said to herself "this is it, this is it, this is it." Given her packed schedule, this client had been at a loss to find the elusive and greatly acclaimed "time for me" window. She hadn't seen, until this moment, that she already had it. Instead of looking for something that wasn't there, she shifted to being grateful for what was. Maybe you, too, could reassess the offerings imbedded in your day. Could it be in the brushing of your hair or in your shaving? Could it be in the running of your bath or in the luxury of your lotions? What if you considered, for now, that this was enough? Or more radically, bountiful? **Could you then join her and say, "this is it"?**

Move Your Hips

Some people really know how to move their hips around when they dance. Apparently, you need to move them independently, like your fingers. A client told me she can do this quite well and feels good when she **dances on all cylinders.** Even more, she spoke of how she would like to do this in all parts of her life. She is not alone in her hip contemplation. Poets write about them, mesmerized by their freedom, magic, and might. Hips go where they want to go. Do what they want to do. They don't like to be held back. Can you imagine allowing them to lead? Can you hear this true alignment calling your name?

Align with Your Merriment

Life invites us into the business of merrymaking, no matter who we are and no matter how challenging our circumstances may be. Therefore, go ahead and fill your life with positive people. The kind who are kind. Who encourage you to be your best self. Go ahead and deliberately fill your life with beauty. The brightest of the light. Take walks near the water, meadow, and woods, even if you have to drive there. Please don't settle. Say "I don't need you" to the old, drab walk down the alley and "farewell" to the person who doesn't celebrate you. Go so far ahead that you, too, use a statement a client taught me **and tell yourself "I am too magnificent for that" when you encounter anything less.**

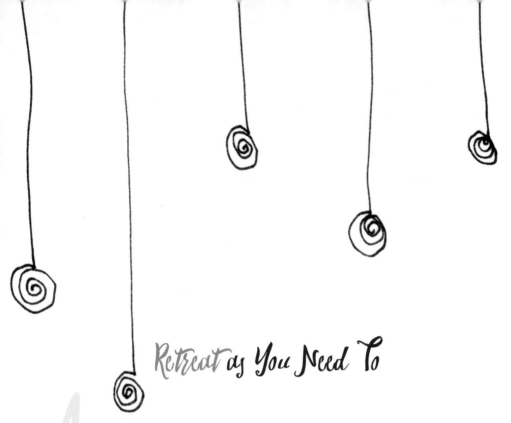

Retreat as You Need To

A client was considering leaving his job but didn't want to talk about it further because he wanted to allow for his defenses. Acknowledging his courageous thought was enough. He didn't want to make plans and go full steam ahead on everything. He was selecting pockets of protection and retreat. Another told me she was working on not listening during her four-hour meetings at work that weren't life-giving. As long as we don't cause harm, might we consider adding this kind of ambition to our self-care list? Where are the places you need to cover your eyes? Where do you need to build a fort with blankets?

Grow into your substantive heart.

Be Substantive

Breathe into being kind. **Grow into your substantive heart.** Embrace your vulnerability, courage, and might. Walk forward with your whole being. Be all this, but please don't be nice. Nice is small. It implies pretending no other layers exist. It can't hold hungry children or fishermen in their boats. Nice arms will break and nice vessels will sink. Only what's real can be strong. Only what's true can hold empathy.

Your Legacy Is Light

You are a creature of the cosmos. The brightest bang and boom are inside you. **Supernovas and massive star explosions shine like ten billion suns and scatter their dust into your body.** No matter who you are, the suffering you have endured need not reduce you. You are not small and dim. You never have been. You are, in fact, bestowed with bounty, favored by the galaxies, made up of matter that matters. It is your true nature. Your legacy is light. Own it, dear brothers and sisters of the stars, and pass *this* on.

Name Your Glory

In the middle of her adult life, a client spoke up to her parents. Her husband called this "monumental," as gathering up her voice and courage had been a long time coming. This became a defining moment that informed her of who she is. A movement from perceived smallness into greater capacity. A rising into glory, solidified in the naming. Our language overflows with words to choose from. Words are made for us. **We can select them to recognize our very souls: heroic, majestic, resplendent, luminescent, and scintillating.** They belong to us all, no matter how full you are of argument, no matter if anyone has ever told you so.

Freedom Is Granted

Imagine being the cat, as a client of mine was. Sauntering toward a warm body, curling up close, and purring. No worries of rejection on that back of hers that flows easily like water. Only obedience to draw near to what causes her purring. Later that same day, she is unapologetic in her independence, knowing it isn't her job to make everyone feel okay. It doesn't even occur to her. She assumes we all operate by these principles and grants this same freedom to all who brush near. **We all need our role models.**

Be Uncommon

I am often asked if a particular desire, feeling, or thought is normal. Whatever normal is, I'm not sure I would know how to recognize it, and I'm not convinced it really matters. Of course, the pain leading up to the question and the person asking matter deeply. The trouble is, the question is a fool's errand. There is no life down this lane. Instead, freedom is more likely found in normal's antonym: extraordinary, uncommon, exceptional, rare, and odd. Try asking your question differently. Get curious if your desire is uncommon, odd, and even extraordinary. Now we are cooking with interesting ingredients and getting somewhere. Now we are talking about you.

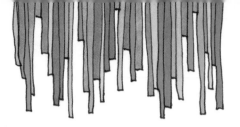

Step Outside the Box

We encounter voices of both perfection and authenticity when we want to create something. These two tongues swing from constricted to free. More notably, they move from not being who we are to being who we are. If we try to create a perfect painting, meal, or self, we become locked up. We get caught up in how others do these things **perfectly** and believe we need to mimic or match them. On the other hand, when we quiet ourselves long enough to listen internally, and draw and cook from there, we loosen and enliven. Then we really take off. To arrive in such a place, **we all need some freedom instruction.** My encouragement to you is to engage in some form of outside-the-box joy. Shake your booty. Hula hoop. Belt out opera in the shower. Jam on your ukulele. Buy a ukulele. Color on your wall. A client told me being a little naughty, having a cigar, and sipping a cappuccino helped loosen up her art making.

46

we ALL
need some
freedom
instruction.

"I just want mashed potatoes and gravy."

Embrace Your Primal Needs

All our needs matter dearly, but sometimes they just boil down to food, drink, sex, and shelter. Transformation and self-actualization live in a house millions of miles away. At the close of a session filled with complex and intelligent reflection about the layers of a client's experiences, I found myself in awe of her revelations. I thought it prudent to gather up her thoughts to hold such a treasure more tightly. Naturally, I then asked this pregnant client how she might summarize the hour. She paused for a moment to consider and then perfectly replied, **"I just want mashed potatoes and gravy."**

Shake Up Your Prescription

Numerous people have said how overwhelmed they feel when thinking of all they need to do in order to feel better: exercise, journal, vitamins, time with good friends, meditation, nature, baths, inspiration books, online classes, breathwork, stretch, garden, support groups, volunteering, and smoothies. While all of this is true and good, so is the story a client told me, through laughter, of cranking up the Barry White tune "Baby Blues" and singing about blue panties. **Sometimes our relief comes in the unexpected and uncomplicated prescription.**

yes yes yes yes yes yes yes yes yes yes yes yes yes yes yes

Heal Your Eyes

"Do you know how beautiful you are? Do you know you can do anything? Do you know how much I love you?" A father met his daughter with these three questions as she came down the stairs each morning of her childhood. Yet here she was in front of me, now an adult, still not believing in her beauty and potential. Still not receiving her father's giant gift that most of us would give our right arm to have received. I wonder how often this happens. Something astounding is right in front of us, telling us who we are. Would you believe me if I told you the answers to these questions are always **yes**? Would you be willing to heal your eyes all the way open?

Raise Your Eyes Up

What grounds you when you are out on the river? When you are in uncharted waters and risk getting in too deep? Into sorrow? Into despair? **Where then is your bedrock shore?** I implore you to raise your eyes up and find it. Quite literally, keep your chin up. It could just save your life. Maybe it is found in your faith, family, or friends. Maybe in movement, meditation, or mountains. Wherever it is, set your sights there. A client was reflecting on his canoeing experience. He spoke of the critical nature of seeing the big picture. The water's ripples and swirls next to the canoe can be deceptive, as they don't clearly communicate when rapids are near. Navigation cues of speed, progress, and ultimately, your safety, are better found by keeping your eye on the land to which you'll return.

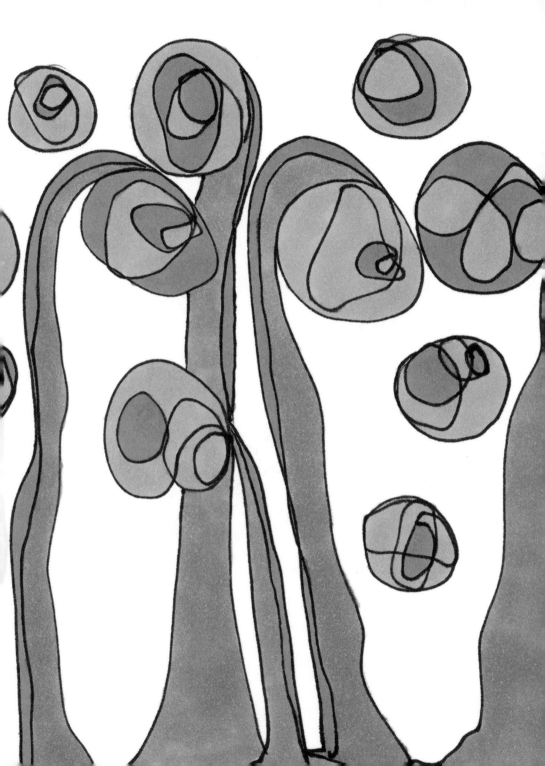

See the *Light* Casting Your Shadow

What stories are you telling yourself, and are they serving your highest good? Is your narrative about being unloved and unappreciated? Then please tell me about how very loved and appreciated you are. Are you finding yourself lost? Then please tell me about being found. While there is room to grieve, it is not a place to pitch our tents and remain. Sometimes our antidote is found in the land of opposites. Our deeper nourishment found in the light that has cast our shadow.

Your Story Is Bigger than Your Shame

A client's pregnancy was unplanned, and she spoke of great freedom from shame in realizing she could **make room in her head for both a mistake and a miracle.** Where are the places in your life that could use such refreshment? Do you find yourself wanting to assert that your life is the exception? That there is no space for both in your circumstances? Might you be willing to consider there is more to your story than you ever let yourself imagine?

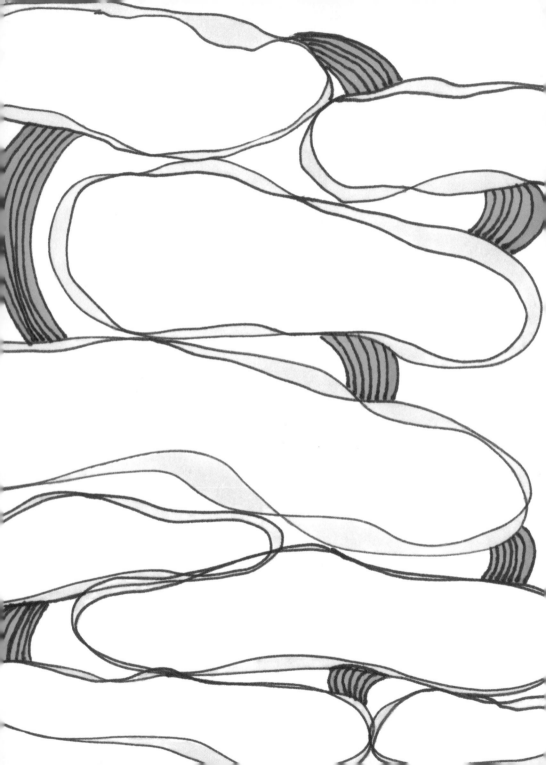

Superhero Powers Are Found in your True Nature

Granted, superhero Clark Kent bumbles around socially and seems to be far from perceptive and mighty. Upon closer examination, he is this and more, possessing powers of flight, superhuman strength, x-ray vision, heat vision, cold breath, super speed, and enhanced hearing. This was the topic of a session with a client who is hard of hearing. Ironically, she is also one of the most profoundly intuitive listeners I know. She hears people in their deepest being. We can all consider what is real within. Is it your nature to be kind, sensitive, artistic, curious, and adventurous? Find your words, and then see and magnify them. Herein lies your superpower: super kind, super musician, super father, and super friend. **We are all called to figure this out, to be exquisite detectives, and then take off and fly.**

Your Love Is Sufficient

A client spoke of her desire to nurture friendships and have her friends over more often as a way of doing so. She had been hesitating, as she hadn't gotten to the task of planting her Rainbow Blend Carrot seeds. She wanted to present food to her friends that would appear worthy and beautiful. As if the orange carrots she had on hand didn't qualify for good company. As if her own love wasn't sufficient. Of course, for us all, **our hearts are always rainbow enough.** This is the arc of our shared story. Our love is always enough. When we get caught up in telling ourselves anything different, it is our deep work to dig in and unearth our true plenty.

you just might
be living
inside an egg
of purpose.

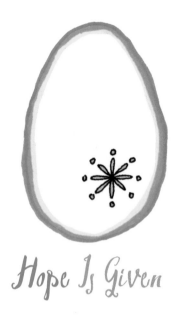

Hope Is Given

It can feel maddening to see a place you want to get to yet be stuck in the land of somewhere else. Hope can appear out of reach. While such hardship is true, so is the possibility that you just might be living inside an egg of purpose. This is the place where you are a tortoise, a frog, or a bird. It is your nature to walk, leap, and fly. Your movement is mandatory. You fight to be born. You persist to break free. You cry out to the shell "let me out" and are met with firm silence. There will be no liberation until you are strong enough to break through. Not even a crack until you are really ready. Hope is serious, freedom fighter. The egg wants to give it to you and thus won't let you go until you can survive and soar on the other side.

Pick Up Your Chisel

The topic of living an authentic life came up with a client who was rearranging her home. She was keeping and highlighting objects and furniture that were consistent with her life and letting go of the rest. You, too, can be a modern-day Michelangelo who spoke of the ease in creating the acclaimed sculpture of **David**. He said he just chipped away at the stone that didn't look like **David**. You, too, can chip away to reveal your distinct you. Chisel away at the parts of your life that don't look like you and honor your true fabulous form.

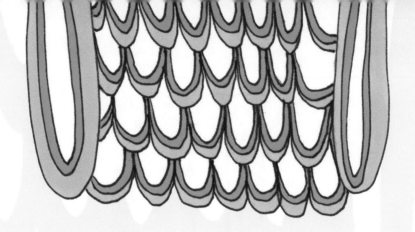

Lean in to Who You Are Becoming

You don't have to stick around for anything, just because you once chose it or just because you are loyal. You can change your major, evolve your friendships, jump ship on your vocation, or take a vacation. While your commitment to stay near to all you have held dear is exemplary, it is not meant to corner you. You are a growing and gallant being. You are no different from children who put down rattles for puzzles and trade up board games for chess. Trust what your life is showing you. Lean in to who you are becoming. **Stay loyal to that and watch your life flow forward like milk and honey.**

Stay loyal

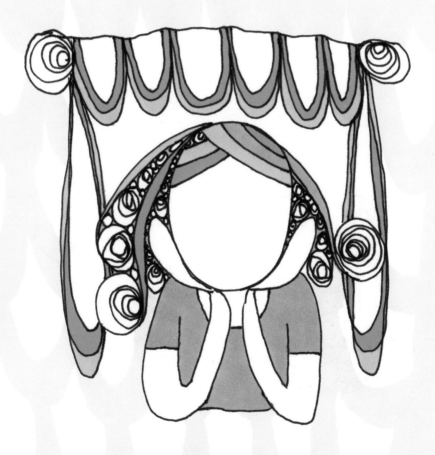

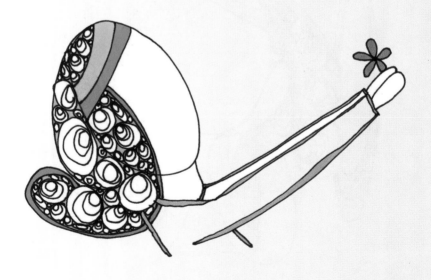

Take In Your Whole Life

One day I was introduced to The Great Green **Okayness**. A client told me about this place where everything belongs and nothing is veiled. It contains all of which we are ashamed and proud. All our anger and all our joy live here without judgment. There is this expanse where we can peaceably see our whole life. If we look real hard, maybe we can all see it. Maybe even, **be it**.

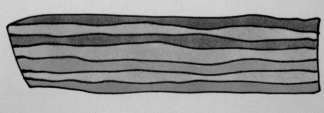

77

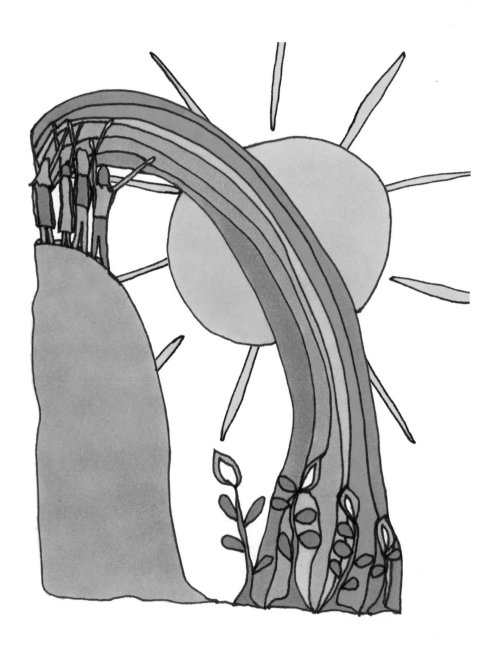

It turns out
that life is
teeming with
help and
rooting you on.

You Are Supported

The smell of smoke was finding its way into a client's home, and he believed it was affecting the quality of his sleep. Ironically, his career involved advocating for the environment. Since he knew NASA had discovered that certain plants, such as the peace lily and florist's chrysanthemum, help clean air pollutants and reduce sickness in space stations, he went shopping. He filled his cart with these greens and brought them home. Might you also need some of these greens? What keeps you awake at night? It turns out that life is teeming with help and rooting you on.

Swing Open the Curtains

Swing open the curtains. Move over the pile of boxes. Let in the sunshine. Make room for summer in the dead of your winter. A bright ball of light beckons. Will you allow for the material of green, light, and water? You can keep summer near: take vitamin D, buy a full spectrum light box, take baths, swim at a local pool, float, visit the conservatory, and plant a patch of grass *inside*. Of course we can all do this. **We can all be a landing strip for butterflies.**

See All That Is Real Inside

We all brim, wax, and wane. Our lives fill, increase, and decrease. Like sand, we are covered with abundant life in the water's waxing and left with holes as it pulls away from our shore. Much of what we hold dear—our health, abilities, relationships, jobs, home, objects, and life—changes and ultimately passes away. A client spoke of filling her hole with good experiences, new adventures, and strong, supportive people. While helpful, she claimed her hole was still a hole. Maybe this is all any of us can do. Stop trying to fill the hole, and instead begin to acknowledge and care for who we really are. **Bear witness to our cavernous tissues, and in doing so, strengthen them.** Listen to them. Learn from them. See them. Their needs are really no different from the rest of you. Like everything else, you need to be seen for all that is real inside.

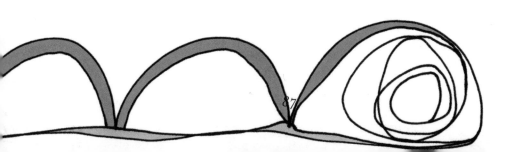

Respond with What You Really Need

A client announced she spent all day Sunday cooking. She was beginning a cleansing diet that would finally heal her gut, and she was in it for the long haul. She was no longer going to address the fringes of her needs, like an occasional massage. This time, she was **going for the core.** This reminded her of how she had decided to major in history in college. She wanted to improve her writing and could think of no other major that required more writing. She said it worked, and she became brilliant at writing. What is the thing you have been dancing around, I wonder? How might everything change if you responded with what you really need?

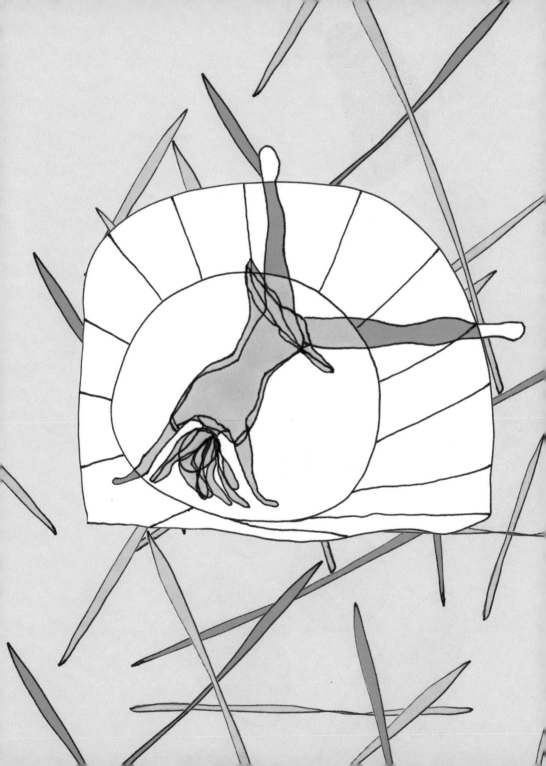

Your Power Is in the Middle

If you are looking to be powerful, you will find it in the middle of your vulnerability, in honoring your core. No strength or substance abides in falsehood. It is an empty room. Maybe consider a new and fitting name for yourself as a way to explore this. I named one client Miracle because her upbringing was painful, yet her life was still astoundingly beautiful. What might your new name be? Dig deep and draw your power from this place. Did you know that **precious metals are so much more abundant in the earth's inner core** than in its crust?

Take Care as You Form and Fire

A ceramicist client expressed his repugnance for mixing the material for slipcasting. It doesn't take much time, but due to its painstaking and messy nature, he was mostly avoiding it. Slipcasting is a technique that helps ceramic artists to keep their clay molecules together and that makes pieces stronger when fired. It turns out there were other helpful things slipping as well, such as meditation and naps. Too busy for it all. Too tired. At times, we all tend to fend off the very things that help us to stay together. What is forming within you right now? What would help keep you together for your firing? **The care you take may make all the difference. Your marvelous molecules are depending on it.**

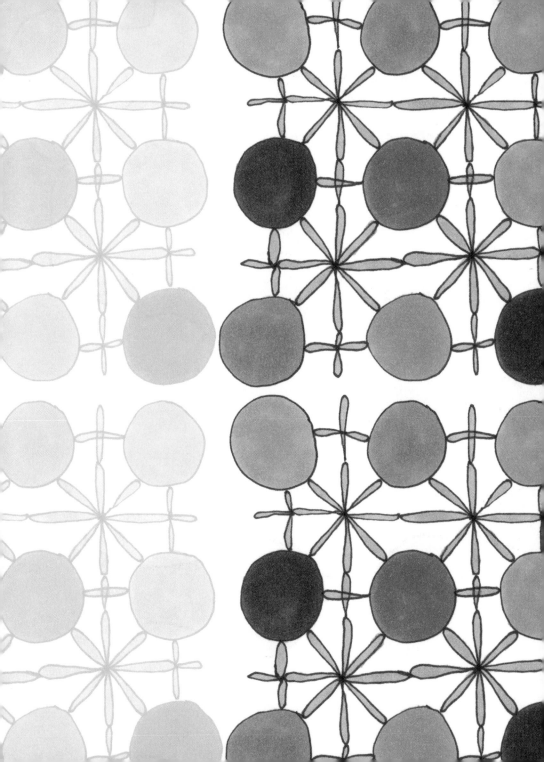

You, Too, Will Rise

Survivors have to work hard to live each day and to make something new out of seemingly nothing. A client told me that no one understands this about her. All she must muster from moment to moment. Without propulsion behind us, it can feel futile to thrust forward. **Stuck in gravity**. Yet there is an alternative called magnetic levitation. This is where great stuff is made. Magnetic fields can make possible flying cars, floating cities, and hovering trains. Big things emerge when we rise above our circumstances. You really can be lifted up. The thing is, **your** star, while set in a storm, might just shake out to be spectacular.

You Are Built for Great Things

The very thing we battle can reveal our greatest magic. An athletic client was unknowingly painting a picture of superheroes as she described her body image. She spoke of her small ankles and lower legs as seemingly out of proportion to the prominence of her upper body. Doesn't this sound a bit like characters from *The Incredibles*? *Superman*? *Wonder Woman*? What might happen if we all woke up one day and realized that we were formed for something remarkable? If we accepted that our makeup wasn't menial, but mighty? Would we up and save a bus full of people about to tip into a lake? Mend our whole world? Restore our entire heart? Magic, of course, is what our chests, thighs, and everything real in us are made for.

What might happen if we all woke up one day and realized that we were formed for something remarkable?

Irrefutable
evidence comes
into play.

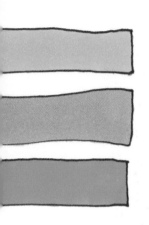

You Will Be Shown that You Are Enough

It can be tempting to believe it is impossible for any of our intelligence and talent to come through to those we love, as our daily lives fall short of perfectly good moods, generosity, and steam. Yet somehow our bumbly love is enough. Love, even though imperfectly given, breaks through and prevails. **Irrefutable evidence comes into play.** A client was wrestling with this very thing when confirming data finally came in. She walked into an airport lobby and her daughter promptly sat at the public piano. Her hands lifted from her lap and began gliding across the keys. She was playing for strangers, for her mom, and now maybe for us all.

Flash with Light

A client told me she needs sparkles—those extra touches that make something magical. The deliberate radiance on a button, glasses, or earring. The dictionary confesses the splendor of sparkles as shining brightly with flashes of light. **Might we reimagine what it takes to stay alive?** What if we claimed food as no more vital than shining brightly with flashes of light? Even Dorothy knew that having sparkles on her shoes and clicking them three times would bring her home.

We all have our **fabulous** ways of being in this world.

Wear Your Crown

A client was at work when a violent person was about to come into the building. She locked the front door within a split second of his entry. She asked me if I knew who she was now, and she added, "I Just Locked the Front Door." Another client told me about soups she makes and serves periodically to people who could use warm nourishment. She claims they are quite good and that she is "The Soup Kitchen Queen." **We all have our fabulous ways of being in this world.** Our moments of rising. It is powerful to identify these roles. Maybe even life changing. We all need to figure out where we can wear our crowns.

Be Present to Your Life Now

Imagine your next birthday as an important appointment. A date with reverie. A call for mad love. Run your finger along wrinkles, with honor and reverence. Read your memoir. Instead of focusing on where you thought your life would be at this point, try on a new set of words: heyday, season, alive, wild blue yonder, eternity, infinity, bloom, boom, fire, fizzle, cycle, circle, coming of age, allow, forgive, thank, and now. Then notice how your new narrative feels. A client felt the power of being present for the now. Because of it, she claimed herself "Mistress of the Universe." The vision of what you thought should be as you turn thirty, fifty, or seventy, is a mirage. **You, too, can be mistress and master.**

You House a Whole Lightshow

Clouds may look cottony and innocent, but they are actually active. Water and ice joust around inside. In their most lively state, they generate lightening. **What comes forward when you allow more space for the clouds within you?** I have been hearing such murmurs in my office. One person is contemplating not wanting just to have fun, but **wild fun**. Another, increasingly disinterested in a tidy, creative life, craves **mad order**. Can you hear the rumblings? **Your** water? **Your** ice? We all house this lightshow. We are all bursting with bolts.

Open to Abundance

As you approach a decision, **first gather your consultation team.** Check in with the little girl or boy inside. Is there joy in this choice? Does it resonate with your beloved dinosaurs, trains, and ponytails? Call up the adult inside. Ring up his or her wisdom. Does a certain direction resound with your highest good? Is it kind? Is it strong? How about the others in there? Angels, fire, and elephants? Do you have their nods? We can all forget to slow down and deliberate. We can impulsively make decisions out of anxiety or default, and then settle for a less desirable result. Instead, please open to abundance. It is your luminous lot. Your destination awaits. Huddle with your whole internal chorus. Your *core-us*. Then go forward and let us hear you sing.

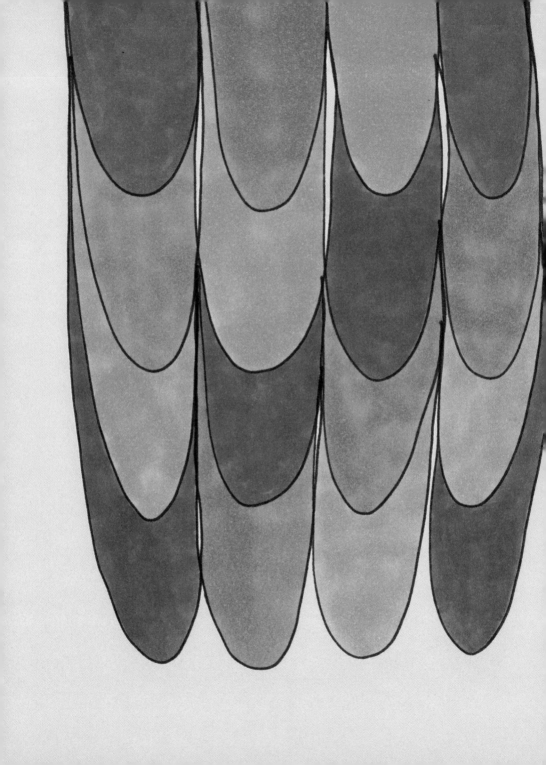

You Belong Here

With a radiant face and winded breath, a client walked into my office. She was fresh from a run and ready for therapy. She drained the water I handed her, and as I refilled the cup, reached for my plant spray bottle and began squirting her face. Her attitude was nonchalant, as if it was no big deal to move through the world. She proceeded like this whole blessed place was her ocean. Maybe she carried secret gills, allowing her to move through the disparate elements seamlessly. **What if we all carry such secrets?** Might you see them if I beamed floodlights into your water? Would such a view resuscitate and free you to move like you belong here?

A Serenade Is Inside

At some point in therapy, many clients say they resume singing. They sing in their heads, showers, cars, and churches. Their notes are heard all over. I have come to hear this as a new season. A bird's spring caroling. Voices returning to their natural vibration. Homecoming is written into our DNA. To true you. Your work is worth all your willpower. A serenade is inside.

Home-coming is written into our DNA.

Combine Our Love

A client noticed it snowed every time we met. These beautiful crystals found their way down from the sky without fail. Something rang a bell in the midst of a mid-April snow session, as we recognized we had been creating a snow globe by coming together. We had cultivated a safe harbor, a bubble, with its own climate. Our own private rain dance, essential for drought. A certain laughter took over us in the knowing. Maybe there is this thing that happens when we gather in safe spaces, where we are seen, heard, and honored. Maybe this is really real. Maybe our combined love is more powerful than you and I have ever dreamed.

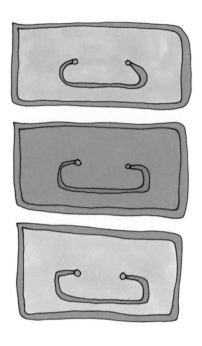

Write Bona Fide Love Letters

A client's husband wrote a list of things that he loves about her. In addition to the classics of funny, intelligent, and kind, the unexpected appeared. Because she is shorter than most, he observed how often she crawls on the cupboards. Because she is an artist, she has interesting things spread about. He liked seeing her shoes scattered around and her art supplies in the oven. She read me the list, which included pages and pages of his actual sight of her, and in it, loving her. We can all make such a list for ourselves by picking up our pens and composing bona fide love letters. **What observations would you include? Are you willing to pick up Cupid's arrow?**

the tumble of
it all becomes
magnificently
hopeful.

Allow for a Tumble of Beautiful Things

It amazes me how one beautiful thing is connected to the next, and as we allow for each thing, **the tumble of it all becomes magnificently hopeful.** One client said she felt moved to put her hand on her chest and say, "hello soul" in order to feel less empty and increasingly well. As she proceeded into the week saying, "hello soul, hello soul, hello soul," she recalled how her thymus gland is located in the same place she was placing her hand. Years ago, she had been encouraged to tap her hand on her chest regularly to stimulate her immune system.

There Is Space for All You Need

Oh, to have one's own closet! Enough space for all you need. A client daydreamed of a whole house for her clothes. What would you fill up a house with? What are you needing? An alcove stuffed with surprises? A foyer of frolicking? Closets abounding with magical unicorns? A pantry of forever enough food? **What if there was enough room for you right now?** What if you proceeded forward, as if this was the truth? What if I did? What if we all broke ground?

You Are Carried

A client said he wants to be like oxygen, carried by the wind and looking for what is next. Can you see oxygen ribboning through rivers, fish, and trees, and all of life, and finally and fully, into and through the vessel of you? This inconspicuous but necessary element wants to carry you. Inspired direction is sketched into your sailboat. **What might follow if you let the most supporting component of your life transport you?**

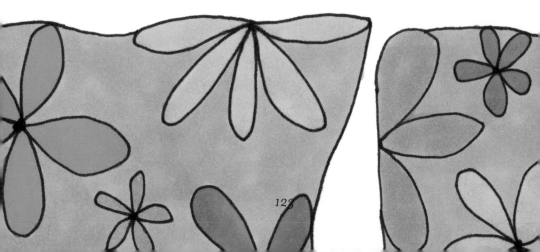

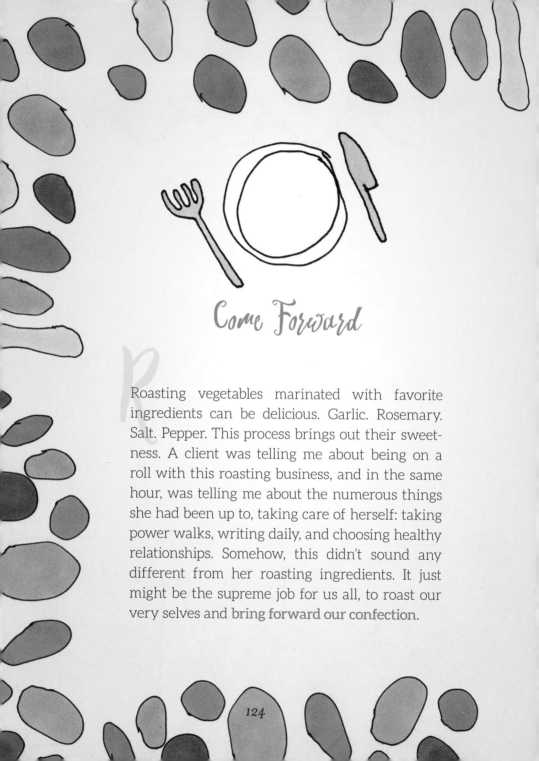

Come Forward

Roasting vegetables marinated with favorite ingredients can be delicious. Garlic. Rosemary. Salt. Pepper. This process brings out their sweetness. A client was telling me about being on a roll with this roasting business, and in the same hour, was telling me about the numerous things she had been up to, taking care of herself: taking power walks, writing daily, and choosing healthy relationships. Somehow, this didn't sound any different from her roasting ingredients. It just might be the supreme job for us all, to roast our very selves and **bring forward our confection.**

Fill the space.
Stretch
into your
symphony.
Deliver.

Allow Yourself to Be Heard

Apparently, a baby grand is more desired than an upright piano. Its longer strings deliver a richer and more harmonious sound. Given its open orientation, the sound also reaches the listener more directly. A client was planning to move and have a piano in her home again. She told me of this clear baby grand selection. It seemed no coincidence that she, too, was living her life more fully. Stretching out her own strings, allowing her powerful sound to be heard. Such is the invitation of our instrument. **Fill the space. Stretch into your symphony. Deliver.**

Don't Leave Yourself Behind

We tend to remember what we leave behind, forget, misplace, and lose—a special keepsake, letter, or a toy. Sometimes we leave parts of our very selves behind. One client recalled the funky white wash jeans she backed off from wearing. Another had stopped playing the piano. Both were drawn to pick up from where they had left off. Both realized there was something of themselves to return to and free. **It is a powerful thing to stay with who we are and build on it.** What are the things buried deep in your closet? Where have you left off? What might happen if you began playing again?

Dress Up

Be subversive. Wear a colorful rumpus. Take pleasure in being the dessert of discord and brouhaha. Stand out. Speak up. Let your Kelly green accessory pop against your chartreuse garment. **Reveal your amusement.** Then step forward and join the world for tea. They will trust you now. They will want to hear what you have to say. A client told me so one day when I was wearing such an outfit.

Turn that Whale Flipper

Can you feel your whale flippers extending out of your deepest oceanic self and steering you where you need to go? Of course, rising up and turning is massive. You have to bring along your whole body. Can you feel all that serious blue water that's flowing the other way when you turn? Can you imagine being so determined to move into it? This is what it feels like when we become caught in waves of sadness and worry. It can feel as if the turn toward more life-giving thinking and nurturing self-care will require heroic strength. Of course, you are right. It will. This is also your water to navigate, dear creature, and **you are powerfully built for it.**

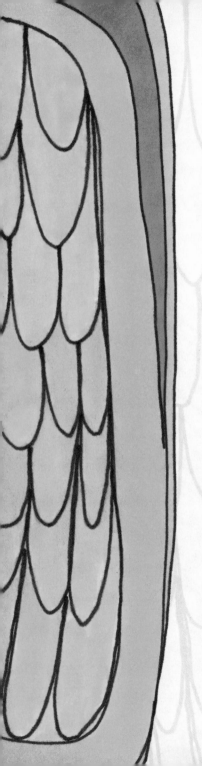

What if
you took

another
look
around?

Love Is Dialing

A client told me she was with friends, and over the course of the evening, held a full-grown chicken. She said the bird allowed her embrace. It made me wonder about the potential hugs our world has for us. About our hunger for touch and affection. About our want for warm weight. About how our desire can be met in the irregular encounter. **What if you took another look around? Where would you newly stretch your love?** Your local animal shelter? Pediatric unit? Nursing home? Neighbor? Person at the coffee counter? A chicken? Beating hearts are everywhere. The hour is here, and love is dialing.

I Can Hardly Wait

Everyone is a drawing and everyone is a poem. A place for imagination to trace. To love. I don't just see your arm, sitting on the couch across from me. I see how my pen would outline it. Your heart appears in acrylics and oils. Words form along your radiant face. Is this what creating produces? Allows our eyes to capture something magnificent in one another? Sculpts us into full vibrancy? If there is any truth in this, then please rush to your pencils. I can hardly wait for you to see you, as I do.

Thank You

I thank all of my clients for inspiring me to write this book and for giving me permission to publish these stories. They have moved me through sharing the real stuff of their heart—speaking soul to soul. It is a superlative gift to be invited into these conversations.

I give special thanks to the client who had the original vision of **The Great Green Okayness** and gave me generous permission to share it here with all of you. She is a testament of how, through authenticity, we can change the world. She wasn't intending on a wide share of the whispers of her heart. She wasn't trying to blast out a kaleidoscope. She simply lived and then told her sacred story to her therapist, and now it's rippling into the land of all over the beautiful place.

I thank my Maker always, for forming me and my dreams, and for imagining up each precious life—of every color, gender, heartbeat, person, animal, tree, water, rock, and flame. I stand in awe of us all.

A big thank you to Wise Ink Creative Publishing, for deeply understanding and supporting my message and my presence, and for generously guiding me the whole way. A special thanks to my publisher Amy Quale, designer James Monroe, and editor Alison Watts. They amplified the best of me and these pages. It is what I most hope for in all our relationships.

A thank you to my photographer Tera Girardin, who was happy to meet me in the thick of The Great Green Okayness, magnificently capturing the cover and author photos.

A thank you to the incredibly talented Nic Askew, who filmed my heart and soul for the book's campaign, and to Emily Eaton, who skillfully edited it with fairy dust to make it just right.

I also thank, with great love, my family and friends for gracing me in my long periods of absence as I continued turning to the quiet, to create. And for giving technical and editorial assistance, helping me find needed resources, for showing up when needed, for believing in me, for kind words, and mostly for loving me. With special mention to Ben, Abe, Sam, Mom, Dad, Awes family, Karen, Holly, Lori, Liv, Carissa, Stephanie, Chrissy, Annie, Cheryl, Sarah, Christy, and Kelly Rae.

Book Club and Personal
Journaling Reflection Questions

1. Your Light

What is your greatest light? How are you holding back from sharing your light? What would it mean to become the bright yellow lion of yourself? What can you newly consider when you think of how stardust is inside your body and your legacy is light? Would you like to make more room for shining brightly? What would be your first steps?

Look for some part of your life where you see a shadow (feeling unloved, unappreciated, lost, etc.) and reflect on the light casting it (reflect on being loved, appreciated, found, etc.).

2. Your Worth

Where could you look for a more accurate mirror reflection of your worth? What is your response to hearing that your heart is framed in gold? What can help you remember that you are precious just as you are, right now? What stories come to mind when you think of yourself as both vulnerable and beautiful at the same time? What affirmations would you like to savor and where are places you could record and keep them?

3. Your Uncommon Magnificence

In what ways are you and your desires extraordinary, uncommon, exceptional, rare, and odd? What kind of instructions could you write for yourself to step outside of the box? Who is included in your internal consultation team (little boy or girl, adult, angels, fire, elephants) and outer team (plants, pets, family, friends, coaches, pastors, therapists) to support all your magnificence?

4. Your Strength

Recall stories of your strength, substance, and might. Like the whale, reflect on how you are powerfully built to meet the serious waters in your life. What grounds you when you are sailing in uncharted waters? How can you both nurture and further strengthen your core? What are the things you want to build on in your life? What are the things you need to let go of?

5. Your Superpowers

What would you consider doing if you realized you were formed for something remarkable? What name could you be crowned with? If you were an animal, what would you be and what does this say about you? If your legs could speak, where would they lead you? What words would you like to newly pull from to recognize your glorious soul: heroic, majestic, resplendent, luminescent, scintillating, a perfectly unprecedented peach, etc.? Consider your true nature and then add the word "super" in front of it: super kind, super musician, super father, super friend, etc.

6. Your Love

Fill in the blank: My love is enough because _____
What would you include in a real love letter to yourself? Where are the safe harbors in your life where you can powerfully combine your love with others? Where can you newly stretch your love into the world? Your local animal shelter? Pediatric unit? Nursing home? Neighbor? Person at the coffee counter?

7. Your Joy

Where do you need to respond with saying "I am too magnificent for that" and make alternative choices that align more closely with your merriment? What songs do you hold inside you? In what ways could you take more pleasure in being the dessert of discord and brouhaha? How can you increasingly reveal your amusement to the world?

8. Your Great Green Okayness

Share some of what you are both ashamed and proud of and then place it into the field of The Great Green Okayness. Ritualize your acceptance of these things. Maybe spread a green fabric over a table and place a symbol of these things there or place written words on the table. Maybe visit a wide-open field and send balloons up as a symbol of your loving acknowledgement. Wear green clothes or accessories for a day and become this place. Carry a green stone in your pocket to remind you. Take time to stretch and breathe deeply. Let this peaceful expanse become you.

Notes

Notes

Notes

Notes

The Great Green Okayness Serenade

"**Green**" by Peter Mayer

"**Beautiful Dawn**" by The Wailin' Jennys

"**September Grass**" by James Taylor

"**This Land is Your Land**" by Woody Guthrie

"**Free To Be You and Me**" by Marlo Thomas

"**Colors of the Wind**" by Disney's Pocahontas

"**Pastoral Symphony**" by Handel's Messiah

"**Greensleeves**" by Mozart

"**Blossom/Meadow**" by George Winston

"**Fragrant Fields**" by George Winston

"**Every Long Journey**" by Ann Reed

"**I'd Like to Teach the World to Sing**"
by The Hillside Singers & The New Seekers

"**It's Not Easy Being Green**" by Kermit/The Muppets

Work with Rachel

Rachel Awes is available for book readings, signings, interviews, and, speaking on the following topics:

- **"The Great Green Okayness":** Select therapy stories will be shared that speak to being seen and knowing: we are loved, have worth, can rise out of difficulty, and, we are not alone.

- **"Diving into Our Lives":** Inspired by the making of her book *diving in* Rachel will reference water as metaphor, as she talks about the stages of a swim and how they awaken us to how beautiful our lives are, when we take the time to listen.

- **"All I Did Was Listen":** Using the seven chapters from her book *all i did was listen* key themes in a transformational process will be discussed.

- **"A Response to the Thirsty Artist":** Four common thirsts will be identified in artists and addressed with encouraging stories and rituals.

Rachel can be reached at: RachelAwes.com.

Speaking Endorsements

"Rachel doesn't speak to you; she hugs you with her words. Taking in her stories and loving nudges feels like a wave of relief; someone really does understand us."

 —Tonia Jenny, senior content developer, North Light Books

"Rachel Awes uses words to reach across a room, lift you up, and hug you tight. She makes you feel as if she is speaking directly to you."

 —Sunny Carvalho, artist, educator, painter of ugly girls, sometimes pretty girls, and maker of things

"Rachel comes across as much more than a psychologist. Her speaking reveals an integration of the dimensions of her true self. She expresses this through her creativity, mingled with soul."

—Sister Lucy Bruskiewicz, masseuse,
Simply Grounded Therapeutic Massage

"Rachel Awes is truly gifted in her ability to bring people together, touch their hearts, and lift their spirit with her warmth and wisdom. She is a rainbow in human form."

—Lori Franklin, artist

"Rachel's joy spills out of her heart like a jar of colorful jellybeans! Such pure goodness and truthfulness in her speaking. It is so refreshing and almost addictive—I want more!"

—Vanessa Kiki Johanning, artist, designer, instructor,
seeker of smiles

"Rachel Awes is a magic maker. She speaks and exquisitely brings out the best in everyone around her. She draws you in with her warmth and authenticity."

—Kim Geiser, artist, maker of happiness

"Rachel is a highly entertaining speaker whose warm, colorful words will resonate with everyone who listens."

—Sallianne McClelland, event director, Art Is You:
Mixed Media Art Retreats

"Rachel really has a way of bringing out the inner joy in people!"
—Sue Georgacas, active older adult coordinator, YMCA

"Rachel's talk was so fun and inspiring! Our group was left buzzing with energy afterward! She was such a hit that she was invited to be the keynote presenter at one of our larger YMCA conferences!"
—Catherine Quinlivan, director of healthy living, YMCA

Other Books by Rachel Awes

all i did was listen tells a story of the progression of wholeness and healing for everyone, through colorful drawings, prose-like reflections, and inspiring quotes from her therapy clients.

diving in is a visual and poetic invitation, using water as metaphor, to dive into the one life that is so beautifully yours.

Both books can be found at rachelawes.com/shop.